**Mountain of Mirrors...Monsters...
Magic...Mystery!**

Whirling around, you discover that the enchanted ice door has a face on this side also. Before you can react, the door starts to scream, "Help! Help! Guards! Intruder inside the mountain!"

You hear the heavy thump of footsteps to your left and gruff orc voices saying, "Let's get the intruder!"

1) If you want to stand and fight the guards, turn to page 93.

2) If you want to run down the staircase, turn to page 39.

Which way do you go? You must defeat the evil in the Mountain of Mirrors and save your village or everyone you love will be destroyed.

Will your quest end happily or will you end up as the monster's slave inside the Mountain of Mirrors?

You Pick Your Own Path to Adventu

BC

MOUNTAIN of MIRRORS

BY ROSE ESTES

Cover Art by Larry Elmore
Interior Art by Jim Holloway

TSR Hobbies, Inc.

For Daniel, Lydia and Max who are the reason for almost everything.

TSR Hobbies, Inc.
POB 756
Lake Geneva, WI 53147

TSR Hobbies (UK) Ltd.
The Mill, Rathmore Road
Cambridge CB1 4AD
United Kingdom

ISBN 0-935696-87-3

9   8   7

First Printing — June 1982
Fifth Printing — March 1983

Printed in the United States of America
Library of Congress Catalog Card Number: 82-50451

ountain of Mirrors is a
DUNGEONS & DRAGONS™ ENDLESS
QUEST™ adventure book. Between the
covers of this book, you will find many
paths to fantasy adventure.

There are many possible choices in this
book; some simple, some sensible, some
foolhardy...some dangerous! All the choices
are up to you. You can read this book many
times with many different results.

Remember, you choose your adventure.
YOU are the adventure.

If you make an unwise choice, go back to
the beginning and start again. There are no
right or wrong choices; only many different
choices to pick from.

We hope you read and enjoy them all!
Good adventuring and good luck!

n Mountain of Mirrors, you are an elf named Landon. You are five feet five inches tall. Although slender, you are very strong and quick on your feet. You are 270 years old. Since elves live to be about 1200 years old, you are still in your early teens in human years. Your hair is a dark chestnut-brown and hangs straight to your shoulders. Your eyes are emerald green. Like all elves, you have elvensight allowing you to see objects in the dark by the heat they give off. You speak a number of languages, including those of orcs, goblins, ogres and halflings as well as the "common" language of humans.

Although you are young and untried as a warrior, you have trained long and hard and are skillful with both sword and dagger.

our adventure begins in the cold, clear dawn of a late autumn morning in your village of Aralia. Mauric, the Chief Elder of the village, has asked his people to gather in the Great Hall for an important meeting.

Speaking in a low, but commanding voice, Mauric addresses his people, "For three months now, no caravans have reached our village. Supplies are running very low. Someone or something has completely cut Aralia off from the Land Beyond the Mountains. We have sent parties of elven warriors to discover what is wrong but none have returned. Soon the great snows will come and our village will perish without supplies. If we are to survive, someone must open the way to the Land Beyond the Mountains so caravans can get through.

"The Council of Elders has met all night in secret session and decided to choose by lot one elf from the village to try to open the way to the Land Beyond the Mountains. The Council feels one elf may succeed where many have not. The name drawn in the lottery is that of Landon. Though as yet untried as a warrior, the Elders feel that Landon's goodness of heart and strength of purpose are more valuable than fighting experience. Landon, step forward."

Ignoring the grumbling from the older warriors, you step forward and say proudly, "Mauric, I accept this mission. Please know that I will do my best."

Mauric continues, "Landon, for your mission, the Council will supply you with a mountain mule and a portion of our dwindling supplies. We are also entrusting you with our greatest treasure, the fabled Sword of the Magus. This sword has many special qualities. It cannot be broken no matter how hard it is struck. At your command, it will throw a clear, golden light over a ten foot area. The Sword of the Magus will hum in the presence of enemies. If you are defeated or slain the Sword will lose its powers. It cannot be used by anyone who is not pure in heart. Prepare yourself, Landon, you leave within the hour."

The hour speeds by quickly as you change from your everyday clothes into a gray suede shirt and pants and a gray hooded cloak lined with silver fur. You put a tiny bone-handled knife into the secret pocket inside your shirt. You lace your tall black leather boots to your knees and begin filling your backpack with supplies. You load it with an axe, a rope, oil flask, some herbal medicine, a drinking horn, a tinder box and torches.

Strapping a silver dagger to your belt and slinging a bow and a quiver of arrows over your shoulder, you prepare to leave. Following a narrow, rocky trail, you leave your beloved village behind, sped on your way by the blessings of family and friends.

Eventually, Aralia becomes lost in the distance. As you climb out of your valley home, rocky peaks tower above you. Snow covers most of the peaks, but a few wear crowns of gray, ancient rock. One peak stands out above the rest. From time out of mind, your people have called it Shanafria... the Mountain of Mirrors. Snow covers Shanafria on all sides and its upper third is shrouded in a sheet of solid ice. When the sun shines, the mountain sparkles like a cold, perfect diamond.

As you approach Shanafria, dark clouds blot out the sun and a chill, piercing wind rises. The path climbs steeply into the roof of the clouds. Several times, your mule pulls back on its reins, reluctant to move forward. You sigh in sympathy. If there were another trail, you would surely take it.

"Mule," you say finally, "sometimes there's no choice and you have to do things you don't like. Stop fussing and move!"

Tucking your head down against the wind, you continue trudging up the mountainside pulling the stubborn mule behind you. The afternoon passes quickly and soon the day grows gray with the coming of night. The idea of spending the night alone on the mountain frightens you, but you have no other choice. Just ahead, you spot a sheltered hollow off the trail. If you hurry, you can make your camp while there is still some light.

You reach the hollow just before sunset. You set up your camp and feed the mule. Then, you set about cooking your own dinner. After eating, you snuggle down into your warmest furs and prepare to sleep. You are so tired that your eyes close almost instantly.

A faint cry reaches your ears. Wide awake, you listen but hear nothing more. You decide it must have been the cry of a nightbird. Settling down, you try once more to get some sleep.

Again, the cry echoes through the valley... louder now. Alert, you sit up and wait for the next cry. You are sure now that it was definitely a voice you heard... the voice of someone in trouble. The cries seem to be coming from the trail. Drawing your sword and slinging your bow and arrows over your shoulder, you creep quietly down to the trail. You see nothing in the direction from which you came.

"Help! Help!" The sharp but still distant cry comes from behind you. Whirling around, you see three elves sprinting full speed down the trail pursued by four ogres. The ogres are nine feet tall with greenish-brown skin, snaggley, yellow teeth and sharp black claws. Each carries a pair of spears.

Seeing the elves' danger, you start to wade through the heavy snow toward the battle.

Close to the edge of exhaustion, the elves stumble more than they run. As you watch, one elf slips on an icy patch and falls to the ground, his weapons clattering away. His companions stop, uncertain, tug his arm and urge him to rise. But he does not move. The elves glance back at the ogres who are gaining on them. Finally, they race on, leaving their fallen friend behind.

One of the ogres picks the fallen elf up by one foot. Struggling weakly, the elf dangles upside down. He pulls out his short sword and strikes desperately at the monster. The ogre only laughs and tosses the elf over the cliff that borders the trail. The elf disappears falling hundreds of feet to the valley floor below.

Still wading through the snow, you glimpse the remaining elves struggle between themselves. The larger elf is weaponless and holds the other by both arms. With a sudden wrench, the smaller elf pulls away and rushes back toward the ogres.

The ogres stand at the edge of the cliff laughing about the elf's death. They are surprised and unprepared for the attack. Sword swinging, the elf is upon them before they realize it.

He strikes first at the ogre who killed his friend, breaking his sword off at the hilt. The dying ogre tries to speak, but crumples to the ground with the broken blade lodged in its body. The elf draws his dagger and flings himself at another ogre. He stabs three times before his new foe can draw its own sword and attack. The other ogres crowd forward to join the fight but there is room on the narrow trail for only one of them. The elf stays out of the range of the wounded ogre's sword and is unable to move close enough to strike it a fatal blow.

Suddenly, out of nowhere, something flies through the air and strikes the ogre on the forehead. The weaponless elf has thrown a snowball to distract the ogre! As he continues to bombard his enemy, the surprised ogre throws its arms up to protect itself. While the snowballs cannot harm the ogre, they do confuse it. The first elf seizes his opportunity, leaps forward and plunges his dagger into the ogre's stomach. Before the body hits the ground, the elf turns and races down the trail.

Screams of rage echo through the valley as the two remaining ogres rush after the the elf. The first ogre grabs a spear. Taking careful aim, it lets the spear fly through the air with deadly accuracy.

The spear strikes the elf, sending him sprawling on the icy trail. He struggles to rise, but cannot.

With a cry of rage, the weaponless elf charges the enemy. The ogre throws its second spear as it runs

The injured elf raises his head wearily and sees the spear flying toward his companion. With a valiant surge of strength, he flings himself between them. Both elves fall heavily to the trail. The weaponless elf struggles to his knees unharmed. But the other elf lies crumpled in the snow with two spears lodged in his body.

"Ulmus! Ulmus!" sobs the weaponless elf.

The ogres roar with laughter at his cries. At the sound of their laughter, the grieving elf leaps to his feet and rushes toward them.

"So you want some of the same, little guy? Keep on coming, elfie. This spear is for you," growls one of the ogres waving a spear.

The ogre's words stop the elf. He stands hesitantly on the trail with no weapons to defend himself.

"What's the matter...chicken? I'll come to you," roars the ogre starting forward.

"Quick, elf! This way," you yell. You are still too far away to help him but are getting closer each second. If you can just reach him, his chances of escape will be better.

The elf hears your words and sprints down the trail toward you. Both ogres shriek in anger when they spot you. Quickly you ready your bow and draw an arrow from your quiver. The elf narrows the gap between you and the ogres are almost within range of your bow. At this distance a bow and arrow is a better weapon than a sword. If you can keep the ogres at a distance, both you and the elf may yet survive this encounter.

Heart pounding, you force yourself to wait until the ogres are within range. Then carefully, you draw back the bowstring and let the arrows fly. They leap from your bow in a deadly arc whizzing through the frigid air toward the ogres.

The first arrow slams into an ogre. It stumbles but continues to lurch forward. Then zock! Zock! Zock! The remaining arrows thud into its body. The ogre stops, takes a faltering step, staggers and falls.

The last ogre kneels by the bloody form of its companion, grabs a fallen spear and rises.

Before you can get off another volley of arrows, the ogre draws back the spear and throws it with tremendous force.

Then with one final growl, it turns and races back up the trail.

You hear a low moan of pain. The spear has found its mark! The elf has been hit. Hurrying up the trail, you kneel at the side of the wounded elf and examine him. The spear has passed through his chest just below his right shoulder.

With a shock, you recognize him as Hallic, an elven warrior from your village, who left with the last party that tried to cross the mountains.

Hallic tries to speak but no words come. He collapses on the snow. Frantically, you tear aside his clothing and listen at his chest. Dimly, you hear a ragged heartbeat; he still lives. Working fast, you cut his shirt away from the wound, and gently remove the spear. Binding the awful wound with pieces of his shirt, you carry the elf to your camp.

Gathering what little wood you can find, you build a fire and wrap the elf in blankets. Then you settle down to keep watch over Hallic throughout the long night.

Around dawn, Hallic stirs and mumbles, "I killed him."

"You certainly did. I never saw such a good shot with a snowball," you reply.

"No, I don't mean the ogre. I mean Ulmus. He was my brother. I killed him. If he hadn't tried to save me, he'd be alive now."

Tears trickle from the corners of Hallic's gray eyes.

"He made the choice," you say in a tear-choked voice. "You must not dwell on his death. Ulmus would not want you to grieve so."

Hallic turns his head, closes his eyes and is silent. Tears continue to trickle down his pale cheeks.

You reach for the horn of herbal medicine simmering at the edge of the fire. Turning back to Hallic, you see he has lapsed into unconsciousness.

All day the elf wanders in and out of consciousness, delirious and feverish. You bathe him with icy stream water, but the fever does not break. You keep trying to get Hallic to drink some of the healing herbal brew, but his restlessness only allows a little of the liquid to drip down his throat. The wound, the fever, and his grief over his brother's death are more than he can bear.

At nightfall Hallic awakens, his gray eyes large and clear. His fever has faded. You reach for the medicine.

"No," says Hallic in a faint voice. "There is no need. The pain has left me and I shall soon be with my brother. I can ask for no more." He fumbles for your hand. You take it and feel his pulse fluttering like a trapped bird.

"Please tell the Elders we tried but there were just too many of them for us."

"Too many of what?" you ask.

"Orcs, goblins, ogres, and even a frost giant," whispers Hallic. "I always knew there was something evil about Shanafria."

"Evil? What evil? Please tell me what to expect."

In a dying voice, Hallic gasps, "Ice caves ...mines...monsters...prisoners. Death! His pulse flickers for a brief moment and then is still. He stares at you with empty eyes, a small smile on his lips.

With a deep sigh of sadness, you prepare to bury Hallic. Throughout the long night you gather rocks. Slowly, you build a rock tomb. At daybreak, you lay the last rock with bruised and aching hands. Hallic is now at peace...and you must go on.

You have difficulty forcing the mule around the frozen body of the ogre. With a bray of protest, it finally leaps forward. Prancing wildly, it dashes up the trail ahead of you. You run to catch it.

The mule has already rounded the boulder ahead of you. Suddenly, it gives a terrified bray. "Stupid mule. Trust it to make a noise like that when we need to be quiet," you mutter to yourself.

You round the boulder and all thoughts of silence leave your mind. You want to cry out in terror yourself. Directly ahead of you, the trail doubles back on itself like a giant C. You stand on one side of the trail next to the braying mule. On your left is the mountain wall. On your right is... empty air.

Forty feet across the chasm is the other side of the trail. Carved into the mountain wall is a cave with the opening framed in ice and snow and sitting at the opening of the cave is an enormous frost giant and a young white dragon.

"Look, Fang!" booms the frost giant, his icy blue skin glinting in the sunlight. "We've got company. Come on, where are your manners? Greet our guests!"

Fang, the white dragon, draws its scaly lips back over long sharp teeth and almost seems to smile. Then, it opens its mouth and belches a cone of white frost that rolls across the chasm. The frost falls far short of you.

"If I've told you once, I've told you a hundred times, you have to practice! You missed an easy shot. Try again!"

The giant seems to think you and the mule are nothing but toys for Fang's target practice. That makes you angry.

While the giant continues to lecture the dragon, you grab your bow and three of your remaining arrows and take aim. Zap! Zap! Zap! The arrows fly across the chasm and bounce off the giant's armor. Even though your shots were well-placed, they have no effect.

Surprisingly, the giant laughs again. "You can't hurt us. You and Fang would make a good team, Tweedledumb and Tweedledumber."

The dragon rumbles and roars.

"Don't like arrows, Fang? Well, blast them again. You're fifty years old. You should be doing better. At the rate you're going, you'll be a hundred before you amount to a hill of snowballs. Now, take careful aim and blast!" cautions the giant.

You grab another arrow. Drawing the bow, you aim and let the arrow fly at the dragon.

"Yirk!" screeches Fang as the arrow strikes its rump. It rolls over on its back digging the arrow deeper into its flesh and making the pain worse. "Yip! Yip! Yip!" it shrills again.

"Don't just lay there screaming," says the giant. "Do something. Are you going to let an elf do that to you?"

As if in answer, Fang blasts forth a great frost cone with a huge roar of anger and pain. Unfortunately, the frost cone strikes the snow and ice hanging above the cave. The roar echoes and bounces off the narrow walled trail where you and the mule stand.

As the echoes of the roar fade, you hear another noise. Softly, at first merely a murmur, it grows louder and louder. Soon it sounds like a thousand dragons roaring. Both you and the giant look upward to see an incredible sight. It looks like the entire mountain is falling! An avalanche! Powdery snow, followed by huge chunks of ice are tumbling straight down the side of the mountain toward you.

"Fang, you stupid idiot! Look what you've done!" bellows the giant. "You set off an avalanche! Get off your scaly bottom and stop screeching. Quick! Get back in the tunnel!"

Fang and the giant are luckier than you. They have shelter. Nothing stands between you and the thundering wall of snow.

You press close to the side of the mountain. Grabbing the mule's reins, you back up the trail the way you came. The mule is quick to follow, almost running over you in its eagerness to escape. You race around the corner just as tons of snow, ice, and rocks crash down behind you on the trail. The thundering, rumbling, and roaring go on for long minutes. The mountain and trail beneath your feet tremble. When the awful noise finally stops, you look around. The trail is gone... the cave is gone... buried deep beneath a mass of ice and snow. The chasm between the two trails is now filled with snow.

If you are to continue, you must dig out the snow-filled trail. It will be difficult and dangerous. One false step and you could plunge from the mountainside to your death.

1. If you want to turn around and go home and ask for help, turn to page 38.
2. If you want to try to dig out the trail and continue on with your mission, turn to page 119.

Standing nine feet tall, the ogre is very frightening. It looks as though it could tear you limb from limb with one hand. You look at its mouth filled with ragged, yellow teeth and remember that ogres consider elves a treat and love to eat them. A long chain dangles from one of the ogres' scaly hands and a huge sword is attached to its belt. You wonder if you can trick the ogre. You are desperately trying to think of a way to do so when you realize the ogre is nearly upon you. It is too late to run.

You wonder if the same trick that fooled the two guards at the entrance will work on the ogre. Hiding your sword and backpack behind a rock, you step out of the shadows and say, "Quick! Tsimmis and Rogor sent me for help. There's an invasion back at the door."

The ogre stops short, looks closely at you and says, "So what... who helps Mang when Mang have trouble? Let them help themselves."

Slowly, you start to back up. "Well, if you don't want to help, that's okay. I'm sure everything will work out. I better get back. Thanks, Mr. Mang." While the ogre's squinty red eyes peer curiously at you, you take a few steps back.

"Where you from?" it growls.

"Oh, I'm new here, sir. I just happened to be at the door. Tsimmis told me to go find help."

"Don't look like a prisoner. Why you run free? Why you still have nice cloak?" The ogre snatches at your cloak but you step back out of its reach.

"Hey! What's going on here? You no messenger. Mang knows!"

You try to edge slowly away. With a rasping clang, the ogre draws its sword and advances on you. You have never seen a blade like it before... solid black and four feet long. When the ogre draws the sword, a curious weakness comes over you. Your knees feel like water. You can't breathe. Your arms feel like they weigh a ton. You are too weak to draw your dagger.

"Met your match, elf. My sword made by evil wizard. Sword named Elf Killer. You don't have a chance. Har! Har! Har!"

The ogre leaps forward and the dreadful blade pierces your cloak. The cold metal slides along your side as you twist away. Your strength ebbs as though you have been fatally wounded. The floor rushes up to meet you and everything goes black.

You awaken to find yourself slung over the ogre's shoulder. You are nearing the line of prisoners. Even though they have been left unguarded, they have not moved. Carefully, you inch your hand toward the dagger strapped to your belt.

Believing you are dead, the ogre has not bothered to search you for weapons. You pull your dagger out of its sheath and plunge it into the ogre's back.

Thud! The ogre drops you to the ground and staggers about, trying desperately to pull the blade from its back. It screams with pain and rage because it can't reach the blade. The corridor echoes with its inhuman shrieks.

"Kill! Kill! You're going to be sorry, little elf. Slice you into little bitty bits." The ogre stumbles toward you its ugly face twisted with hatred. It swings its sword menacingly.

You watch in terror as Mang approaches. Too terrified to move, you cover your eyes. There is the harsh sound of metal striking rock, a heavy thump, then...silence.

Cautiously opening one eye, you spot the ogre lying on the ground staring at you. You open your other eye. The ogre is still lying on the ground. It has not moved! The ogre is dead!

You have killed the ogre. Its dreadful sword, Elf Killer, lies broken and powerless on the ground beside it.

All your strength returns in a rush as you leap to your feet. Excited, you run to the motionless prisoners.

"Hey! Let's go! I killed the ogre! Follow me. I can get us out of here!"

The prisoners do not move. Thinking that they do not believe you, you rush back to the body of the ogre and search it for the key to the chains.

"Look, I found the key! I'll have you free in no time." You dash about, freeing one prisoner after another. Still, there is only silence from them. They stare stupidly at the ground with their arms dangling loosely at their sides. When the chains fall from their necks, they begin walking slowly and silently down the dark corridor.

"Where are you going? Wait! Stop and talk to me. What's going on?" you yell at them. The prisoners do not stop until they have reached the tiny cells where they wait patiently to be let in.

"Listen. You're free. Let's get out of here!" you plead.

Not one prisoner turns...not one prisoner speaks.

"What are you? A bunch of zombies?" you say grabbing the arm of one of the prisoners. The arm feels like rubber, cold and lifeless.

Your excitement and hope die as you look at the silent line of prisoners. Realizing that only death will free them now, you back away down the corridor.

You give the prisoners one last, sad look back and see them still standing patiently in front of their cells. You can do nothing more for them. Your village still depends on you and you must continue.

1. If you choose to return to the ledge, run to the staircase and take your chances, turn to page 39.
2. If you choose to investigate the corridor you passed earlier, turn to page 129.

Your party spreads out through the forest looking for dead mushroom stalks. You drag the stalks back to the river's edge. Collecting leather vests from everyone in the party wearing one, you carefully slice the vests into strips and then you construct a crude raft by weaving the leather strips, your rope and the tough muchroom stalks together. You hack down several live mushrooms to complete the raft and to use as oars for the dangerous crossing.

At last your raft is ready! Everyone gets aboard. Nigel is last, grinning nervously as he tests the footing on the floor of the raft. "Doesn't leak, does it! Can't stand wet paws, you know. Is it safe? How do I know we won't sink? Dear, oh, dear...maybe I should stay on dry land?"

Nigel worries and frets until finally you pull a large mushroom cap from the raft. "Here, sit in this. It will keep your fur nice and dry." Nigel steps gingerly into the mushroom cap twitching his whiskers nervously. Before the lynx can change his mind, you push the raft away from the bank.

The wild current grabs the raft and whirls it downstream. Using the mushroom stems as oars, you fight the current and the ice floes. Slowly you edge your way across the river.

The other shore is within sight when a gigantic ice floe appears out of the gloom headed directly for the raft. You and your companions row as fast as you can.

The ice floe catches the edge of your raft and tilts one corner up until all of you are clinging to the very edge of the raft. Grinding, tearing and howling noises fill the air. With a body-jarring thump, the raft crashes back down in the water. As the ice floes whirl wildly past, you discover that two of the mushroom stalks at the end of the raft are gone. You all paddle wildly to get the party to shore before the raft can sink beneath the icy waters.

Making a quick head count, you see that everyone is safe and accounted for except Nigel. It must have been he who howled. When the raft tilted, the mushroom cap with the lynx inside must have slid off into the waters. As if in answer to your unspoken question, a great, unhappy yowling comes out of the darkness from the other bank. You row as fast as you can toward the sound.

The raft strikes something hard and wedges between two rocks. Scrambling off the half-submerged raft, a curious sight meets your eyes. You start to laugh uncontrollably. Soon humans, halflings, and elves are all roaring with laughter at the sight of the wet and bedraggled lynx. Nigel still sits in the mushroom cap but is most definitely not happy.

"I don't see anything funny," sniffs Nigel. "Some people don't like heights... some ignorant souls are even afraid of cats ...I simply don't like water. It's perfectly understandable."

Water drips from his nose, ears and body forming a large puddle inside the mushroom cap. Nigel steps out of the soggy cap, shaking each foot violently. He then proceeds to lick himself dry.

You walk to a large rock by the edge of the shore and peer over it to scout out the territory. What you see makes you freeze with fright. A vast plain stretches before you. A few mushrooms still stand but most have been chopped down and used for the fires that dot the plain as far as you can see. Camped around the fires are scores of goblins, ogres, and orcs gobbling their evening meal.

"Landon, I don't think we stand a chance of getting by them," whispers one of the halflings. "There's just too many monsters."

One of the humans nervously fingers his knife and says, "We'll never get through that camp. Let's leave now before they find us. There's got to be another way."

As you are discussing your situation, loud cheering and yelling breaks out from the monster camp. Peeking over the rock again, you see a terrible sight. A feeble, old halfling has been pushed into a clearing in the camp. Shaking with exhaustion and fear, he stands surrounded by the mocking monsters. Some are staring upward and shouting, "Here, Fang. Dinner time. Here, Fang."

An orc tosses a spear to the halfling and a goblin throws in an axe. They taunt him by yelling, "Pick them up! Entertain us, you skinny runt! Let's have some action!"

The feeble halfling continues to stare at his feet rather than picking up the weapons. Slowly he falls to the ground in a heap next to them. Bored, some of the monsters start to pelt the unfortunate prisoner with small rocks and bones.

"Get up!" cry the monsters. "Fight for your life! Do you want to be dragon chow?"

A great wind stirs the air and the flapping of huge wings drowns out any sound of the screaming monsters. The dragon is coming.

1. If you choose to leap out and attempt to rescue the halfling, turn to page 143.
2. If you choose not to rescue the halfling and escape instead, turn to page 102.
3. If you choose to push the raft back into the river and try to cross to the other side, turn to page 135.

You've already tried force and the only result was a bruised shoulder. You'll never succeed in melting an enchanted ice door.

You decide to leave. Taking your axe out of your backpack, you start to cut footholds in the ice.

"Goodbye," chuckles the door. "Do drop in again."

It takes a long time but eventually you climb back up the snowy trail. You rest for a while to regain your strength and then start out toward your village.

You will have to tell your story to the Elders. Perhaps you will be able to try once more to reach the Land Beyond the Mountains. Maybe there will still be time...

You have reached The End of this adventure. Go back to the beginning for another adventure.

Looking at the mass of treacherous snow, you decide the way is too dangerous to travel. Slowly you trace your way back down the mountain. You avoid looking at Hallic's tomb when you pass. You feel he would not have approved of your choice.

When you arrive home, the people of Aralia stare at you. You greet a few, but they avoid looking at you and hurry away.

The Council of Elders greets your story with grim silence. Mauric, the Chief Elder, says in a trembling voice, "Landon, I'm sure you did your best. We will have to try to find some brave, strong elves to accompany you and dig out the trail...that is if the storm lets up."

You look up in surprise and, running to the window, see that snow has started to fall. The heavy, wet flakes are sticking to the ground. Winter has arrived!

You have reached The End of this adventure. Go back to the beginning for another adventure.

You run down the staircase and into the billowing clouds. The clouds protect you from being seen. It would be easy to fall over the icy edge so you know you must be careful.

You hear sounds. The cloud muffles them but you can make out two voices.

"Kvetch, me hate this post," says a gruff orc voice.

"Be quiet, Kimmel. All you ever do is complain," snarls the second harsh voice.

You stop and think. You have to make a decision.

1. If you choose to try and talk your way past the guards, turn to page 73.
2. If you choose to attack the guards, turn to page 41.
3. If you choose to run away before you are discovered, turn to page 91.

Nigel says, "You chaps run along. Possibly I'll catch up to you later."

Hoping for the best, your party jumps into the wildly swirling water. The river is choked and swollen with ice and dead monsters. You climb on a chunk of ice and cling to it. The frigid waters carry you outside of Shanafria.

The ice chunk slams against a larger ice floe in the water and bounces off toward shore. When it reaches the rocky bank, you jump off. You are cold and exhausted. Leaning back against a rock, you close your eyes wearily and drift off to sleep secure in the knowledge that you have beaten the evil in Shanafria.

When you have rested, you will make your way home to Aralia. You will be proud to tell your people that the evil in Shanafria is no more.

You have reached The End of this adventure. Go back to the beginning for another adventure.

Your elvensight allows you to creep through the cloud layer and get close to the orc guards. Before they know you are there, you have slain the orc standing closest to you. The other orc whirls around searching for the attacker hidden in the clouds.

Lowering your head, you rush at the orc and try to butt it off the stairs. Its feet shuffle on the ice as it scrambles wildly to catch its footing. It is not successful. Screaming horribly, it plunges over the edge.

It was not an honorable fight but orcs are not honorable enemies. Had they caught you, they would have shown you no mercy.

1. If you choose to go back up the staircase, turn to page 84.
2. If you choose to continue down the staircase, turn to page 76.

Cautiously, you enter the dark passage. Your elvensight shows that no one is near. Sword drawn and ready for battle, you creep down the corridor. You travel for about 20 minutes and encounter nothing. Other dark and silent passages open off this main corridor.

At last, the corridor opens out into a large stone room. Twenty small, cell-like units have been carved into the damp walls.

Each little cell contains a tattered blanket and a grimy bowl. The openings to the cells are heavily barred. There are small doors near the stone floor. You wonder what unlucky creatures live in the tiny cells. You hear sounds coming from the corridor, but you cannot make out what they are.

1. If you choose to investigate the sounds and the cells, turn to page 95.
2. If you choose to run away, turn to page 99.

You can just see the bottom of the steps when you hear and feel great thudding footsteps. Soon you see a fifteen foot frost giant striding toward you through the mushroom forest. Its ice blue body is heavily muscled and covered with silver and leather armor. A shaggy mane of blonde hair tumbles over its shoulders. Hawk-like amber eyes peer out from beneath frosty eyebrows. A blonde mustache flows into the beard that nearly covers its broad chest. Your knees start to shake. Pressing against the icy wall, you hope it won't see you.

The giant slashes its way through the mushroom forest with an enormous double-edged battle axe. Suddenly, you recognize it as the frost giant you met on the ledge outside.

You wonder why the ground is shaking. The frost giant is a huge monster but it is not large enough to make the ground shake under its feet. Suddenly the giant turns and points a huge stubby finger upward. "Go home! I command it. Never have I met such a dumb dragon. Go home now!" A young white dragon walks behind the giant. It's Fang!

Fang doesn't listen to the giant's command. Instead, it walks forward and stretches out on the ground laying its scaly head across the giant's feet. Whimpering softly, Fang looks at its master with huge, sad eyes.

The giant is not pleased. "Get up, you dumb dragon. Stop following me. You're the most useless excuse for a guard dragon I've ever seen. Stop that whimpering. I can't stand it. I wonder how many orcs I could get for you on a trade-in?"

The giant kicks the dragon. Fang yips and yelps even louder, making the giant even more angry. Reaching down, it grabs the sniveling, whimpering Fang by the scruff of its neck and tries to make it stand. Instead, Fang goes limp and collapses like a wet noodle.

As the giant reaches for its club, Fang rolls over on its back. All four sharply-clawed feet wave in the air. Fang cries loudly. Finally, the giant loses its patience and gives Fang a whack with the club. Fang springs angrily to its feet and blasts a spray of frost directly at the giant. The frost cone covers the giant with ice from head to toe. Attacking a frost giant with frost is like pouring water on a duck. It's useless and only makes the giant angrier. It smacks Fang with the club and kicks it on its scaly rump. "Get home or no young maidens for dinner."

The last threat seems to affect the dragon. After a few half-hearted frosty bellows, it flaps its great wings and lurches clumsily upward. Fang flies away heading in the direction of the ice pillar. You wonder if this is where the giant and the dragon live and resolve to be very careful if you travel that way.

The giant turns around and starts walking toward the staircase. You were so interested in watching the giant and dragon that you foolishly forgot your own safety.

You look around frantically for a place to hide. You see nothing but the stairs, the ledge behind you and some strange clumps of blue-white ice against the wall. You are trying to figure out what to do when you hear a tiny, crackly voice say, "Elf! Over here. Hide thyself behind us!" The voice comes from the strange ice clumps.

At any moment, the giant will see you. You have several choices:

1. If you choose to run away, turn to page 100.
2. If you choose to hide behind the ice clumps, turn to page 49.
3. If you choose to fight the giant, turn to page 81.
4. If you choose to talk to the giant, turn to page 97.
5. If you choose to surrender to the giant, turn to page 92.

You decide to trust the tiny voices and take their offer of help.

One of the voices crackles again, "Over here. Duck down behind the ice." You slide between the ice clumps and flatten yourself on the ground behind them. Only seconds later, the giant stomps up the staircase past you.

You carefully stand up and look around trying to find who saved you. You see nothing but the strange clumps of ice. "Where are you?" you whisper.

"We are here!" answer many tiny voices. You still can see nothing. But then, the strange clumps of ice begin to move. They glide slowly toward you until you are ringed by the strange clumps. They look like ice but they talk and move. What can they be?

As if reading your mind, the largest knob glides forward, stops directly in front of you and says, "We are the Guardians. We have been the Keepers of Shanafria from all time. We are the elements of the earth. We are here to protect and use wisely the Earthen Fires your people call diamonds."

The Guardian continues his story, "We hollowed out the mountain and built the great dome and the ice pillar. For centuries, we were alone... building, mining and existing peacefully with nature.

"Then, the monsters came. At first only a few... then more and more. They brought death and destruction to our peaceful mountain. They care not for the beauty of the Earthen Fires. They only collect them out of their foul greed. They are not satisfied with a portion of the Earthen Fires. They want all Shanafria holds. To accomplish this, they ambush helpless travelers on the mountain passes and force them to rip our mountain to pieces mining for the Earthen Fires.

"There is only one way to stop the monsters from destroying our mountain and taking more helpless travelers prisoner. We must destroy Shanafria and begin again. If thee are willing to help us, we will help thee. If thee refuse, thy chances of escaping harm are slim."

You realize the Guardians are your best chance for survival.

"Guardians, I will gladly help you. Our goals are almost the same. Please tell me how to accomplish your mission."

"The way is difficult and dangerous," says the largest Guardian. "It will require bravery. Thee may not survive." A chill of fear runs down your spine but you do not speak. The Guardian continues.

"The pillar is the key. Thee must bring it down. Once it falls, the entire mountain will collapse, burying all the evil beneath it. After a time of healing, we will once again rebuild the mountain and live in peace once more.

"We have used our Mirror of Souls to read thy thoughts. We know thee to be both honorable and trustworthy. That is why we will trust thee with the Mirror of Souls... our most precious possession."

You hear a crackling sound and part of the Guardian shatters and falls to the frozen ground. Embedded in its body is an enormous diamond as large as your head. A ray of sun filters down from the dome and is caught by the huge gem. The light divides into a million bright beams so brilliant that you stare at the diamond as though hypnotized.

"This is the Mirror of Souls of Shanafria, the most beautiful of all Earthen Fires. With it, we can look into the hearts and souls of others to see their strengths and weaknesses. We also use it to call other Earthen Fires to the surface.

"Thee must find thy way through the mushroom forest, across the wide silver river, and into the ice cavern by the side of the whirlpool. Travel in darkness and try to avoid the many wandering monsters.

"When dawn comes, thee must use the Mirror of Souls to catch the rays of the sun. Thee must direct the beam of light at the ice pillar. If thee can hold it long enough, the ice pillar will melt and the dome will collapse. Remain in the cavern during this time and thee will be safe.

"One thing thee must promise us, once thee has destroyed the dome, thee must leave the Mirror of Souls in the cavern. It must remain in Shanafria. Thee may then leave with our blessing and the knowledge that thee has helped to destroy a reign of evil.

"Guard the Mirror of Souls with thy life. Thee are now the last Guardian...the last hope."

With fumbling fingers, you reach for the gem. It is cold and heavy in your hands. With great care, you wrap it in a soft blanket and tuck it away in your backpack. "You have my word," you promise. "I will do my best. If I rid Shanafria of evil, I will also save my own people. Farewell, Guardians."

Taking a few steps, you turn around to wave goodbye but all you see is the staircase, the ice wall and a few clumps of ice. The Mirror of Souls feels heavy on your back. A whispered voice says, "Goodbye, young elf. May thee have good luck."

The mist grows heavy with the fall of night. You find the foot of the mountain and locate a dark opening in the rock. Looking inside, you see nothing but hear sounds coming from the rear of the cave. Discovering a tunnel leading from the cave, you follow the sounds. You creep down the tunnel for a long time and find yourself at the entrance of a huge room. Tied up in the room are many elves, halflings, and humans all of whom look angry and unhappy.

Your heart jumps with excitement when you recognize three elves from your village. They were among the last party to try to reach the Land Beyond the Mountains. If you could free the prisoners, you would have help with your mission.

It will not be easy. Squatting around a meager fire are four goblins cooking their dinner. Their short swords lie within easy reach.

"Well, this bunch should last awhile," rasps one goblin gruffly.

"Maybe. Don't last long down here," says another. "Think it's the cold and dark that kills them off?"

"No, it's the rotten food," says the third goblin.

You draw the Sword of the Magus and leap into the circle of prisoners and goblins. The magic blade hums and crackles. The astonished goblins look up, their hands and faces smeared with grease from their meal. They stumble to their feet in confusion and grope for their weapons.

Not giving the goblins a chance to arm themselves, you swing the magic blade. Two goblins are struck down almost immediately. The remaining two reach for their swords but their shoddy blades are much shorter than the Sword of the Magus.

Metal clashes on metal, and one goblin's blade breaks off at the hilt. Before it can grab another weapon, you run it through. The last goblin stares at its fallen friend. Pulling its green lips back in a snarl of hatred, it turns and runs out of the room into the dark tunnel leading into the mountain.

The goblin disappears quickly. You decide not to follow but to rescue the prisoners instead.

Quickly, you use the Sword of the Magus to cut the ropes that bind the prisoners. They are overjoyed to be rescued and ask you many questions. Speaking quickly, you tell them all you know.

"We must destroy this evil. Until we do, innocent elves, humans, and halflings will continue to be seized by the monsters to work in the mines. We must stop them."

"If we decided not to try and stop them and simply ran away, we would not be safe for long. Whether we want to or not, we must do our best to destroy Shanafria as the Guardians ask.

"We cannot help those already trapped in the mountain. It is more important to save our loved ones in the villages around Shanafria. None of you is obligated to go on the Guardian's mission with me. You are free to try to leave the mountain. Speak now if you wish to leave."

The firelight shines on the faces of the rescued prisoners. One of the elves from your village named Desval steps forward, "Landon, you can count on us. We've had some dreadful times since we were captured. We know what will happen if the evil in the mountain is not stopped. We are with you."

"Thank you, Desval. Come then... this place is dangerous. We must leave quickly. Let us equip ourselves as best we can."

You search the dead goblins. In addition to their swords, you find daggers, an axe, and a spiked club. You put your own dagger and axe in the pile and distribute the weapons to the group. Worried that the goblin who escaped may return with reinforcements, you urge everyone to hurry.

Your party files silently out of the room with you in the lead. You reach the entrance to the cave and look out. Night has fallen. The dome of Shanafria is hidden by clouds. Although the mushroom forest blocks the river from your view, you can still hear its powerful roar.

"Stay together," you order. "If we are separated, we may never find each other. Be careful and be quiet."

You and your party enter the mushroom forest. Some of the mushrooms are normal size, but most tower above your head. Some are as big and flat as tables. Sometimes you have to climb over great piles of dead mushroom stalks that lie like fallen tree trunks. Only your keen elvensight allows you to pick your way through the misty forest.

Near the edge of the forest, Desval clutches your arm, "Look over there, Landon! Did you see it?"

You look in the directon Desval pointed but see nothing.

"It was there, a large animal lying on top of that mushroom," stammers Desval.

"It's not there now. Maybe you saw a shadow?" you suggest.

"No! I tell you. I did see an animal. It was looking directly at me. One minute it was there and the next it was gone!" exclaims Desval.

The others in your party cluster around you. "I see it," says a halfling, pointing to your left. You turn and see a large cat-like animal lounging on top of a mushroom. As you start toward it, it vanishes before your eyes.

There is a gasp of fear and wonder from your party.

"There! Look at it. It's a blink-lynx!" cries Desval.

The animal appears in front of you lying lazily on top of a large mushroom. The blink-lynx begins to groom his silvery-gold, spotted pelt as your party draws closer. You draw your weapons ready to attack. The lynx doesn't react; he simply yawns and continues to groom his fur. However, his brilliant golden eyes never leave you.

"You look a bit silly, you know," says the lynx. "I'm not the least bit hungry. Why don't you put away your weapons? However, if you're hungry and plan on eating me, then I'm afraid I must decline the honor." The lynx blinks out and disappears.

"No, we don't want to eat you. We just want to get across the river. Please come back!" you yell.

The lynx blinks back and says, "In that case, maybe I'll stick around. This could be quite entertaining." He stretches lazily on the mushroom cap, then leaps to the ground beside you.

"It gets rather boring around here. There's absolutely no one around to talk to except those mangy monsters. I have great fun with them, blinking in and out. Drives them crazy. But, you know, even that gets old after a while."

"Who are you and what are you doing here?" you ask the giant cat.

"Silly elf. Anyone can see I'm a nobly handsome blink-lynx in the prime of my life. My name is Nigel. Believe me, I should be anywhere but here. You've heard that curiosity killed the cat? Unfortunately, that goes for blink-lynxes too, even smart ones like myself.

"One day, I was out strolling in the mountains when I came on an orc. Now orcs taste perfectly foul...filthy personal habits, you know. I could never lower myself to eat one! But it is great fun leaping about, roaring and frightening them half to death. Orcs are so entertaining. They have absolutely no sense of humor. Only this time, it didn't quite work out the way I'd planned."

"I followed the orc into an ice cave. Well, the next thing I knew, I was sliding down an ice chute. My fur got all messed up!

"I ended up by an enchanted ice door that said to me, 'What's the matter, kitten? Lost your mittens? Now, don't begin to cry.' Then that wretched door laughed at me. I admit I might have been a bit flustered, but I certainly wasn't crying.

"Finally, the door got tired of teasing me and opened, saying, 'Run along, little kitten, try to find your mittens in here'."

The lynx continues his tale, "It's terrible being in here. It's full of monsters. There are elves, halfings, and humans here, too, but after a week they act like a bunch of zombies. I'd give anything for a nice, juicy rabbit," Nigel says wistfully.

"If I ever get out of here, I'm going to have to wash my mouth out with soap for a week to get rid of the taste of monsters and mushrooms!"

Nigel blinks in and out nervously and says, "I'm sure there is a way out of here if only we can get across that river. If I help you, will you take me along?"

You answer Nigel quickly before he disappears again. "I'm sure you will be a great help to our party, Nigel. Tell me, do you know how the monsters get across the river?"

"There's a guarded bridge," he replies. "You have to know all sorts of complicated passwords. The monsters examine everyone very carefully. No prisoners are allowed to cross the river."

"Why do the monsters guard it so heavily?" you ask.

"It's because of all those silly diamonds and the ice pillar," the lynx says. "The monsters store all the diamonds that the prisoners mine at the base of the ice pillar. There are simply heaps of them! I can't for the life of me understand all the fuss about diamonds. After all, you can't eat them!"

"How many monsters guard the bridge and the ice pillar at night?" you ask.

"Except for the monsters guarding the prisoners, every monster in the mountain is over there at night. There's also a white guard dragon. I don't think it ever sleeps."

"I just know there has to be a way across the river, but that's your job. You figure it out."

"Let's all go to the river and have a look," you say. "Then we'll try to figure out a way to cross it."

Walking in single file, you head toward the river. The sound of rushing water grows louder as you push your way through the mushroom forest. Standing on the bank of the river, you watch the murky water churn past. Large chunks of ice spin and bob around in the current. You talk with your friends about the best way get across the river.

1. If you choose to try to swim across the river to the far bank, turn to page 98.
2. If you choose to leap from ice floe to ice floe until you reach the other side, turn to page 101.
3. If you choose to build a raft from mushroom stalks and float across to the other side, turn to page 30.

You decide it would be foolish to honor a promise made to the Guardians. They couldn't have survived the falling dome. Packing the Mirror of Souls in your backpack, you lead your party across the glistening ice field.

The footing on the ice is very treacherous. When you are almost halfway across the ice, a knob of ice pops up out nowhere. You trip over it and fall into a deep ice pit. The sides are too steep and slippery to climb. You feel cold, but it doesn't really bother you. You start to feel sleepy and your eyelids feel too heavy to stay open. Snuggling closer to the ice wall, you yawn sleepily and close your eyes. Dimly, you hear your friends calling your name, but you are too sleepy to answer.

Out of nowhere, you hear a shivery, whispered voice say, "Thee failed to honor thy promise, Landon. Sleep... now. Sleep... forever."

You have reached The End of this adventure. Go back to the beginning for another adventure.

Quickly, you light your torch. Fierce blue flames shoot up and water begins to drip from the ceiling. The air grows warmer. Holding your torch before you, you stride to the door.

"You wouldn't dare!" shrieks the door.

"Want to bet. I'll melt you in a minute if you don't open up immediately!" you shout.

Water streams down the face of the door making it appear to be crying. Its features begin to soften and melt. Its bushy eyebrows droop over angry eyes. A drip trembles from the tip of its nose. The mustache hangs limply over the sagging mouth. The features start to blur. Water is now ankle deep in the small room and the walls and ceiling steam with mist.

"Help! Don't melt me. I'm really a good fellow. I'm only doing my job. If you stop right now, I'll let you in," begs the door.

"Okay, door. I'll stop. But you better let me in and no tricks!" you say.

"Get that torch away from me and I'll let you in," says the door.

Creaking on icy hinges, the door swings open just wide enough for you to squeeze through. Cold air blasts you, blowing out your torch as you press through the opening. You are bathed in a cold, brilliant light that streams down from the crystal dome far above you.

A narrow ledge branches to your left and right. Directly in front of you is a broad staircase lightly dusted with snow. The staircase descends into a layer of clouds and you cannot see where it leads. There can be no doubt about it...you are inside Shanafria, Mountain of Mirrors. Turning around, you discover that the door has another face on this side.

"Ha! Ha! Didn't know I was two-faced, did you?" the door says smugly. "Well, you got in. Let's see how much good it does you." The door starts to scream, "Help! Help! Guards! Intruder within the walls!"

You hear the thud of heavy footsteps to your left. A gruff voice yells, "Tsimmis! Rogor!"

1. If you choose to stand and fight the guards, turn to page 93.
2. If you choose to run down the staircase into the cloud layer, turn to page 39.
3. If you choose to run along the ledge to your right, turn to page 91.

The corridor is dark and might be full of dangers. At least, you know something about orcs so you decide to try to trick them.

You hide your backpack and sword under your cloak and rumple your hair, trying to look like a harmless messenger. Rushing up to the two guards, you say, "Quick! Tsimmis and Rogor are holding off an invasion back at the door. They sent me to get help."

The two orc guards squint at you for a minute with their mean, piggy eyes. Then, they rush off down the tunnel to help their friends. You wait until you are certain they are gone, then hurry on your way.

Please turn to page 42.

You approach the two orc guards. They are armed with swords, daggers and carry shields. They look cold, bored and unpleasant, even for orcs.

"Hi, guys," you say casually. "Tsimmis sent me to deliver a message. I need to go down the staircase."

"Oh, yeah. What's the password?" says one of the orcs.

"Password? Gee, what is the password? It was on the tip of my tongue but I seem to have forgotten it. Couldn't you let me pass just this once without it? Tsimmis will be so angry if I don't deliver this message," you say.

Both orcs laugh wickedly. "Too bad, elfie," says the taller orc. "Tell you what. We help you because we like you. Wouldn't want Tsimmis to get angry with his nice little elfie."

Nervously, you shift from foot to foot, waiting to see what the guards are going to do.

Suddenly, the taller orc lunges at you and grabs you tightly around the neck. Grinning horribly, showing its ragged, black teeth, it says, "We take you back to see Tsimmis. Then you can tell Tsimmis how you forgot the password. Tsimmis probably won't get too angry. We soon see if you are telling the truth, elfie."

"Oh, no! Please don't take me back to Tsimmis," you squeak. "I'm sure I'll remember the password in just a minute."

The orcs ignore you. Glad for any excuse that will take them away from their boring post, they head back up the staircase, dragging you by the scruff of your neck.

"Tsimmis," bellows the taller orc. "Got a present for you!" Instantly you are surrounded by grinning, piggy orc faces.

"Your messenger forgot the password," says one of the orcs.

"Messenger?" Tsimmis asks. "I sent no messenger. Thanks for catching this intruder for us. I'll see you get extra food tonight."

Seizing a dagger from one of the guards, you stab Tsimmis in the heart. It falls dead at your feet with a terrible splat.

Before the other guards can recover from the shock of seeing their leader slain by an elf, you are sprinting down the corridor like the wind.

Please turn to page 75.

You run down the dark corridor looking desperately for a hiding place. At last you see something with your elvensight...a crack in the rock wall. A crack just wide enough for an elf to slide through, but not big enough for any monster to force its way through.

The crack seems to extend forever. It must be a natural fissure formed when Shanafria was created. Squeezing your body sideways in the crack, you follow it for a long time. It slopes gently downward and gradually widens. You feel fresh, cold air on your face. Suddenly, you realize it is night and you are outside Shanafria on the trail back to Aralia.

You begin the return to Aralia. Once you are there, you will gather an army of elves. Together with your knowledge of the secrets of the mountain and the battle skills of the elven warriors, you will return through the secret passageway to defeat the evil in the Mountain of Mirrors.

You have reached The End of this adventure. Go back to the beginning for another adventure.

You continue down the staircase and entering the cloud layer, you meet no more orcs. You are very cold. Only a little light manages to flicker through the clouds. The footing is dangerous and the staircase seems to be endless. Even with your elvensight, you have a hard time seeing through the cold mist. Occasionally, you catch glimpses of dark openings in the rock. Ledges circle the walls on four different levels. Sometimes, you see figures moving on the ledges, but you cannot make out who or what they are.

Beneath you on the cavern floor, giant mushrooms rise eerily through the mist. In some places huge clumps of the mushrooms have sprouted making the cavern look like a nightmare forest. A broad silver river slithers across the cavern floor. Huge chunks of ice spin end over end in its powerful current. Even from here, you can hear the river's roar.

One feature of the spectacular landscape stands out above the rest. In the center of the cavern is an enormous ice pillar. It rises from the floor of the cavern and soars into the clouds. You try to estimate how big it is... it would take at least twenty elves holding hands just to encircle the base.

You can just barely see the end of the staircase. It looks like a path leads from it to the mushroom forest, the river and the mysterious ice pillar beyond. To your right, there is a ledge leading around the side of the mountain. A dark opening is visible at the end of the ledge.

1. If you choose to follow the staircase, turn to page 43.
2. If you choose to follow the ledge and enter the dark opening, turn to page 42.

You command the Sword of the Magus to light the area. Clear, golden light floods the grim corridor, blinding an ogre and a pathetic line of prisoners. Surprised, the ogre stumbles backward and fumblingly draws its own sword, an evil black blade four feet long.

"Elf, you met your match. My sword made by evil wizard. Sword named Elf Killer. You don't stand a chance," snarls the ogre, swinging Elf Killer in a wide, whistling arc.

Your blade was made to throw light and to have extra strength. Elf Killer has the opposite effect. It casts a black light and absorbs light and strength from anything in its path. As Elf Killer sweeps near you, you feel your strength ebb. Your sword's power suddenly fades, casting only a dull glimmer. As the ogre advances, swinging the deadly Elf Killer before it, you step back. The light from the Sword of the Magus flickers and dies. You are terribly afraid.

The ogre towers above you, crooning wickedly, "Good little elfie." Taking the Sword of the Magus from your trembling fingers, it leads you to the column of chained prisoners.

You struggle weakly against the ogre, but it easily takes all of your weapons and supplies. You become one of the pathetic prisoners you had hoped to rescue.

When the ogre returns Elf Killer to its sheath, your strength returns with a burst. You leap at the ogre only to be pulled up short by the chain around your neck. The ogre laughs, "Settle down. Save strength. Need it here to stay alive. Har! Har! Har! Get moving." Saying that, it gives you a well-placed kick that sends you sprawling toward the little stone cells you passed earlier.

Now you are a prisoner! But you won't be a prisoner for long! When the ogre took your weapons, it didn't find your knife hidden in its secret pocket. You will work the knife out of the secret pocket and free yourself from your chains. You will still learn the secrets of Shanafria and defeat the evil living there. You promise yourself that!

You have reached The End of this adventure. Go back to the beginning for another adventure.

Stupid dragon or not, you don't want to be its dinner. You look around frantically. Next to you is a wall made of boulders; some of them are larger than you. You get the glimmer of an idea. With luck, maybe you can defeat the giant.

Putting the point of the Sword of the Magus behind a large boulder, you quickly pry it from the wall. The boulder comes loose easily, wobbles uncertainly, then topples onto the staircase. It teeters on the edge of the steps for a moment, then crashes from step to step gathering speed as it goes. By the time it reaches the bottom of the staircase, it is barrelling straight for the frost giant. If you are lucky, the boulder will flatten it flatter than a pancake.

The grinning frost giant stands with hands on hips. It chuckles with glee as the boulder picks up speed. With a thundering laugh, the frost giant catches the boulder easily in both hands. It lifts the boulder above its shaggy head and hurls it straight at you.

Dodging to your left to avoid the boulder flying at your head, you slip and fall down the staircase. The giant holds out its huge hands and catches you easily. It yells triumphantly, "Dinner, Fang!"

You have reached The End of this adventure. Go back to the beginning for another adventure.

You turn and plod back up the staircase, hoping that the guards have left. Stepping out of the cloud cover, you are immediately spotted by the seven orcs who now guard the door.

The door screams, "There's the intruder! Catch that elf!"

Drawing the Sword of the Magus, you try to fight but the orcs fall on you and seize you. They take your weapons and bind you with a rough cord. Behind you, the door bursts into a hideous off-key victory song.

Taking the end of the cord dangling from your neck, one of the orcs gives it a sharp yank jerking you to your feet like a dog. They march you down the ledge.

You hang your head and pretend to be terrified. Secretly, you are plotting and planning your escape. When the orcs captured you, they neglected to find your knife hidden in its secret pocket. You will use the knife to cut your bonds and sneak away from the guards. Somehow, you will make your way out of Shanafria and back to Aralia.

It will be difficult to convince the Elders to raise an an army but you are sure you can do it. You will return to Shanafria to rid it of the evil that lurks within.

You have reached The End of this adventure. Go back to the beginning for another adventure.

Hoping to cross to the other side, you continue on, leaping from ice floe to ice floe. You see the other side and shout excitedly to your friends. But they cannot hear you. Looking downriver, you see a horrible sight.

The current churns into an enormous circle. It's a gigantic whirlpool! One by one each of your friends is being sucked into it. The ice floe you are riding flies around in wide circle. You are now on the outer edge of the whirlpool and starting to swirl into its eye.

You need all your energy just to cling to the ice floe. The frigid waters numb your body. The suction from the whirlpool draws you closer to its eye. Knowing the floe is doomed, you plunge into the icy water. Your muscles stiffen immediately in the cold water but you still manage to swim for the shore. Suddenly, Nigel calls your name from the shore and you try to swim toward him.

You swim as hard as you can but your muscles are too stiff to keep you afloat much longer. The current pulls you back toward the whirlpool.

Holding his cat nose as high above the water as possible, Nigel blinks-in beside you. Again, the current pulls you toward the whirlpool.

"My dear, Landon," Nigel says through chattering teeth, "allow me to be a hero and save you." The lynx turns around in the water and says, "Grab my fur. But do be careful. Don't pull any of it out! Can't stand that patchy look, you know!"

You sink your hands deep in his heavy pelt and he swims strongly for shore. Soon, the lynx crawls up on the shore with you still clutching his wet fur.

"I hope you appreciate this," Nigel gasps. "Because I wouldn't jump back in that river to save my own mother, let alone an elf." Shivering and muttering complaints under his breath, Nigel begins to groom his fur.

You sit next to him in glum silence. You are alive, but you have lost your friends, your weapons, and the Mirror of Souls in the river.

You have reached The End of this adventure. Go back to the beginning for another adventure.

You take your axe and begin to hammer in the door. Ice chips fly everywhere.

The door begins to scream, "Stop that!"

You keep on hammering at the door. An eyebrow breaks off, then part of the nose, and the chin. The door stops screaming.

You take a step back and look. The face is gone, smashed into splinters, but the door is still solid. You have not weakened it at all. You collapse on the floor and stare angrily at the door.

Water begins to trickle down the front of the door. The water drips, freezes, and then drips some more. Before your eyes, new features take form...bristling eyebrows, hawk-like nose, sneering mouth, and angry eyes. The new face smiles evilly and says, "You cannot destroy me by force, little elf. As long as there is water and cold, I am eternal."

As long as there is water and cold...you wonder. Has the door, itself, given you a clue how to defeat it?

Please turn to page 69.

Pulling out the Sword of the Magus, you rush toward the monsters. You succeed in slaying two of them but, unfortunately, two others lurk nearby. They push you against the wall and take your weapons. As they stuff you into a large, smelly leather sack, you hear one of them hiss evilly, "Should we take it to the mines or should we eat it for dinner?"

Sitting all scrunched up in that smelly sack, you vow that you haven't come this far to be a slave in the monster's mines or tonight's main course. Slowly and carefully, you work your knife out of its secret pocket.

Cautiously, you start to make a small hole in the bottom of the bag. You work at the hole until it is big enough for a foot to go through... then your leg... then your whole body.

Heart racing, you think of your loved ones in Aralia and, taking a deep breath, you leap from the bag and sprint down the dark corridor.

You hear outraged shrieks of fury from your captors and the heavy thump of footsteps following you.

Please turn to page 75.

To win the battle, you must know how many enemies you will face. You don't want to run down the icy staircase into clouds that could hide unknown dangers. You decide to take the ledge to the right.

You leave the shrieking door far behind as you sprint along the ledge. Ahead of you is a dark corridor opening off the ledge. Beyond the corridor stand two orc guards with their backs to you. They are not yet aware of your presence.

1. If you choose to try to avoid the guards and slip into the corridor, turn to page 96.
2. If you want to try to trick the orc guards, turn to page 72.
3. If you want to attack the guards while they are still unaware of you, turn to page 90.

You know you can't attack a frost giant and live. You decide to surrender and try to talk it into keeping you alive.

Hoping for the best, you cry, "Mr. Giant, I come in peace. I mean you no harm."

With a look of astonishment on its ice-blue face, the giant skids to a halt and bellows with laughter, "What a day! First, that dumb Fang and now a rude elf!"

Still laughing, the giant picks you up and gives you a shake. All your weapons clatter to the ground. It slings you over its shoulder like a sack of flour and strolls off toward the ice pillar.

You beat your hands on the giant's broad back but it only chuckles and says, "How would you like to have dinner with Fang... with you as the main course?"

You feel a sharp jab in your side...it's the knife you hid in the secret pocket of your shirt! You slide it out of the pocket and stick the giant in its tender earlobe. The giant lets out a startled squeal. It grabs its injured ear and drops you to the ground. Before the giant knows what's happening, you are on your feet and running like a deer down the dark corridor.

Please turn to page 75.

Armed with swords and spears, five armored orc guards appear on your left. You draw the Sword of the Magus and back away. The ugly monsters advance confidently. You slay two of them immediately.

Realizing that you are too tired to defeat the remaining three monsters, you start running down the corridor looking for a hiding place. You hear the heavy thud of the orcs' footsteps pelting after you. Their bloodthirsty cries of fury are deafening in your ears. You must find a place to hide or you will surely perish and all hope of survival for Aralia will die with you.

Please turn to page 75.

Pressed against the frosty stone wall, you move slowly down the corridor listening intently.

You hear blows, cries, and the rattle of chains. A rough voice growls, "Get up, lazy elf, or you'll be tonight's supper. All you do is cry for food and blankets, but you won't work for them." You hear more blows and cries of pain. More chains rattle and the footsteps draw closer.

You edge forward until you see an ogre carrying a large sword and leading a ragged line of human, elf, and halfling prisoners. The dirty and exhausted prisoners are linked together by a chain that runs from one thin neck to another.

You watch and shudder. You want to help the poor creatures. But if you get killed trying to help the prisoners, you will fail the people of your village. It is a hard decision to make.

The ogre stands with its back to you. It screams at the pathetic line of prisoners, "Hurry up! I want dinner."

You back up and hide behind a boulder until the ogre and its prisoners pass.

1. If you choose to run away down the other corridor, turn to page 129.
2. If you want to try to fool the ogre, turn to page 23.
3. If you choose to attack the ogre, turn to page 79.

You do not want to fight if you can avoid it. Moving quietly, you press close to the wall and edge your way up to the dark opening. So far, your luck has held. The orcs have not heard you. Wrapping yourself tightly in your elven cloak, you dart into the dark corridor.

Please turn to page 42.

You decide to talk to the frost giant. Stepping forward boldly, you raise your hand in a sign of friendship. "Greetings, Sir Giant," you say. "I come in peace. Please listen to me."

The giant is in a very bad mood. "Who cares if a puny elf comes in peace? I'm not interested in hearing any dumb elf message. Drop your weapons and come down here. Anyone as stupid as you deserves to be a dragon's dinner."

1. If you choose to surrender to the frost giant, turn to page 92.
2. If you choose to fight the frost giant, turn to page 81.
3. If you want to run away, turn to page 100.

Most of the party vote to jump into the river and swim to the other side. You instruct everyone to tie their weapons to their belts and everyone jumps into the river. Too late, you realize the current is too strong and swift. Your people weigh too little and worse than that, the water temperature is near freezing. Quickly you shout to the party, "Get back to the shore. We can't make it across. We'll have to try another way."

Everyone manages to swim back to shore. You are cold, battered and exhausted. But in spite of your exhaustion, you are happy. Everyone has made it back to shore safely. You decide to rest a while and then try something else to get across the river.

Leaping down from the top of a giant mushroom, Nigel says smugly, "I hate to be an 'I told you so,' but I did warn you. Now, get yourselves dried off and let's get going. I want to get out of this miserable place. Think of some other way to get across the river."

1. If you want to try to get across the river by leaping from ice floe to ice floe, turn to page 101.
2. If you choose to build a raft from dead mushroom stalks and float across the river, turn to page 30.

You listen for another minute then, hearing nothing, continue down the corridor. Leaving the cells behind, you walk down the dark tunnel, hand on the hilt of your sword. The Sword of the Magus begins to hum, at first just a murmur, then louder and louder. You command it to be silent. Now you hear the sounds of footsteps, cries and the rattle of chains.

As you press against the damp wall you hear the sound of blows and someone yelling, "Get up, lazy elf. Always crying for food and blankets, but won't work for them."

It is obvious to you that elves are being beaten and held prisoner by a vicious monster guard. The sounds are coming closer so you will soon find out what is going on.

1. If you want to run away and explore the other corridor, turn to page 129.
2. If you want to see what is coming, then try to attack it or trick it, turn to page 95.
3. If you want to try to free the elves from their captor, turn to page 79.

Frost giants are big, mean and too terrible to fight. You decide discretion is the better part of valor and run away.

1. If you choose to take the path along the ledge to the left and slip into the first dark corridor, turn to page 42.
2. If you want to run up the staircase, hoping the guards have left their post, turn to page 84.

It seems to you that with so many ice floes choking the river, your best chance is to leap from ice floe to ice floe until you reach the other side.

You leap from one floe to the other as they bob past. The speed is dizzying and the chunks of ice tilt dangerously. The roaring grows louder. With horror, you realize you are being drawn into a huge whirlpool rather than working yourself to the other side.

1. If you choose to try to get back to the bank where you started, turn to page 132.

2. If you want to continue on and hope for the best, turn to page 85.

You decide that there is no way you can rescue the halfling. The attempt would only cause your own deaths.

The dragon slowly flaps its way to the ground. More monsters crowd their way to the pillar to watch. They call out, some cheering the dragon on, others jeering at the halfling to fight.

You creep over the edge of the icy bank and slip away from the camp. There isn't much chance of the monsters spotting you... all eyes are on the hapless halfling. You hear the insane screeching as the monsters bet against each other.

You see Fang lumbering into the sky with the halfling clutched in its claws. You dare not stop to watch. The monsters will be returning to their dinners and you could be caught.

You and your small party race across the enemy camp, dodging from one rock or mushroom clump to the next. Luck stays with you, and you succeed in slipping off into the bleak darkness that stretches beyond the monster camp. Even though you are now out of sight of the camp, fear keeps you moving.

At last, you collapse with exhaustion. You can run no farther. Heaving great ragged breaths, humans, halflings, and elves lie together on the frozen ground until their energy returns. For once, the lynx is doing something of value. He scouts ahead looking for new dangers that may lie in your path.

You gather around the trunk of a giant mushroom, resting and sharing your small supply of food. Suddenly a shadowy creature leaps into your midst. Drawing your weapons, you leap to your feet.

"Really," says Nigel, "not a very warm welcome for a brave scout! Be careful with those beastly blades. You could rumple my fur!" With a glad sigh of relief, you put your weapons away and gather around the lynx to hear what he has discovered.

"The land is simply littered with monsters," says Nigel. "They all speak of a great raid to take place tomorrow. The monsters are no longer content with small amounts of gems. They want all the diamonds and they want them now!

"From what I can figure out, the monsters plan on attacking three of the closest towns. They will capture all the village inhabitants. All those who are able will be forced to mine the diamonds. Those who are weak will be sport for the monsters' amusement or dinner for Fang. The towns in danger are Polycanthus to the north, Aralia to the east, and Cambria to the south."

Cries of rage and grief break out as members of the party hear the names of their villages. Your heart grows heavy when you hear the name, Aralia... Jewel of the Mountains... your home!

"To avoid the death and destruction of all we hold dear," you say, "we must act quickly. We must not fail." There are cries of approval from the other members of your party. You hurry off anxious to fulfill your mission.

The rest of the night passes like a nightmare. With the aid of the lynx as a scout, your elvensight, and the light from the Sword of the Magus, you thread your way through the mass of sleeping monsters. Monsters of every description lie on the ground in snorting, muttering heaps. Shortly before dawn, you and your party spot the cavern the Guardians told you about. It will be difficult to reach.

The cavern is no more than a deep hole in the side of Shanafria. It is located directly above the far edge of the whirlpool. The entire river of melting ice and snow drains into the seething pool. It has such a terrible suction that even the largest ice floes are sucked in by the current. Grinding against each other with terrible groaning noises, they whirl and spin in ever smaller circles. Finally, they are swallowed up by the yawning black eye of the whirlpool. To fall into the river would mean certain death.

Looking closely, you can see a narrow trail of brittle rock and ice clinging to the side of the mountain that leads from the plain to the surface of the cavern. If you are careful and lucky, you should be able to reach the cavern before morning. With Nigel in the lead, you creep carefully along the trail. Your faces press against the rough rock, and your fingers strain for hand holds.

As you scrape your painful way along the ledge, it becomes more and more difficult to travel. A fine mist rises from the whirlpool and coats the trail with a slippery dew. Suddenly, there is a scream of terror... a human, heavier than the other members of the party, loses his grip and plunges into the river below. He is lost forever.

The sure-footed lynx has found shelter in the cavern. "I say, come along. Why are you lazing about on that ledge? It's much more cozy in here."

Nigel's words give you a sudden surge of energy. You force yourself along the last few feet of the icy ledge and fall exhausted onto the floor of the cavern. Leaning over, you reach out to pull the rest of the party to safety.

You have reached the cavern in time. You cannot see the ice dome through the cloud layer, but the clouds glow with the pearly pink of early dawn. You can see the entire plain below. Orcs and goblins scurry around gathering up weapons and arming themselves for battle. Quickly, they put out the last few fires still burning. It is a frightening sight. If you do not succeed in stopping the monsters now, your loved ones will be lost.

A bright ray of sunlight pierces the cloud cover and strikes deep within the cavern. Now it is obvious why the Guardians directed you to this spot. It is one of the few places under the dome where sunlight can penetrate the dense clouds.

Acting quickly, you place your backpack on the ground and gently lift out the Mirror of Souls. Placing it so that it catches the rays of sunlight, you focus the brightest beam of light on the center of the ice pillar. Members of your party gather rocks to make a secure base so the Mirror will stand alone if you are attacked.

Watching anxiously, you stand at the edge of the cavern. At first, nothing seems to be happening. Then a muttering can be heard. It grows louder and louder.

The monsters on the plain look around in confusion. They don't understand what is happening. At last, hearing shouts from their friends camped closer to the pillar, they look up. The monsters have followed the brilliant beam of light back to the cavern where you stand. A loud shout goes up as you are spotted by the monsters. They do not yet understand what the beam is or what it is doing. They do understand that you are somewhere you shouldn't be.

Raising their weapons high, several groups of monsters scream threats and start toward you. You glance nervously toward the ice pillar. You cannot tell if the beam is working or not.

A tremendous roar goes up as the frost giant slides down the pillar and calls the army of monsters. You are too far away to hear what it is saying. However, you can see from the giant's frantic gestures that it understands what you are trying to do. A great cry goes up from the monsters. They move in a mass toward the cavern.

A sea of monsters surges toward you, intent on stopping you from completing your mission. If the beam does not do its job, you will only be able to hold the monsters off for a short time. There are only a handful of you against thousands of them.

Spears hurled by the first wave of the mob clatter against the mountain's walls. The only approach to the cavern is the trail by which you came. The monsters cannot attack directly because the whirlpool roars below the cave. They are too heavy to climb the fragile ledge. Even if they could, they would be targets for everything you could throw from the cave. So far, your perfect positon has saved you. But more and more spears and arrows are bouncing all around you. Every moment is precious. Every second that the beam can do its work must be gained. You cannot see any changes yet, but you do think you hear a faint cracking sound.

There is no doubt about it now. You do hear a cracking, rumbling sound. The monsters hear it too and turn toward the pillar. They begin screaming and pointing upward.

Reflected light is bouncing off the pillar and is lighting up the clouds dramatically. They boil violently, charged with a strange energy. Within the dome, the sky churns.

All at once, you hear a sharp crack! An intense flash of lightning rips through the clouds and strikes the plain in the middle of the monster mob. The monsters panic and run back and forth crashing into each other.

There is no escape for them. An increasing number of lightning bolts tear the sky, stabbing into the plain, leaving death and destruction in their wake. You and your party cower against the far wall of the cave. You are safe from the lightning, but it is a terrifying sight to behold. Thunder crashes and echoes back and forth inside the walls of the mountain.

The sounds of shrieking from the plain bring you once more to the edge of the cave.

"Look, Landon!" cries Desval, clutching your arm tightly and pointing at the river. When you climbed the ledge to the cave, the river and whirlpool were twenty feet below. Now, the river is swollen with huge chunks of ice that have fallen from the pillar. The ice bobs up and down in the murky water that now laps at the edge of the cave.

In its rapid rise, the river has swept many monsters into its flow. They struggle helplessly for a few minutes, then sink beneath the churning waters. Other monsters, still struggling, are sucked into the raging whirlpool.

A chill runs down your spine as you realize that you may soon be in the river. The frigid waters have now spilled over the edge of the cave and are rushing over the floor. The cave will flood in a few minutes drawing all of you and the diamond into the turbulent waters.

1. If you want to leap into the water and try to swim to safety, turn to page 40.
2. If you want to leave the Mirror of Souls in place, crowd to the back of the cavern and wait out the flood, turn to page 137.
3. If you want to remove the Mirror of Souls and hope the waters go down, turn to page 115.

You hastily knock the Mirror of Souls off its rock base. There is no immediate reaction, but the water slowly goes back from the edge of the cavern. The lightning lessens. Too afraid even to move, you huddle at the back of the cavern.

A great roar brings you trembling to your feet. The frost giant stands across from the cavern bellowing with rage. Fang sits eagerly at its feet. The giant screams, "Get them, Fang!" With that command, Fang lurches awkwardly into the air.

Fang flaps its clumsy way across the deadly whirlpool and reaches into the cavern with its large claws. You attack Fang fiercely but are not able to harm it.

Fang grabs all of you in its claws and delivers you to the giant, who glares down at you and says, "Try to destroy my world? Well, it didn't work. I don't know what to do to repay you for this mess, but I plan to think of something truly horrible. This I promise you. I do thank you for bringing me the Mirror of Souls. I've searched for it for a long time. I plan to put it to much better use than you did!"

The giant takes away all your weapons and stuffs everyone in a large leather bag. Tied firmly inside the bag, you can hear the giant ordering the monsters to clean up the damage caused by the flood.

The giant shakes the bag and gives it a brutal squeeze. It says direly, "Comfortable in there, little ones? This is just the beginning."

You don't see how you will ever get out of this fix. Suddenly, you feel a sharp jab in your side. You wonder what it could be. Then you remember... your small knife! You remember how carefully your mother sewed the secret pocket into your shirt.

You cautiously pull the knife out and start to make a small hole in the bag. You manage to make the hole large enough for you to slip out. You warn your friends to be quiet, then creep quietly into the darkness. Moving like a shadow, you scout the area for monsters. Everyone appears to be occupied cleaning up the flood damage. You give the signal and all your friends pour out of the bag and join you.

You whisper to them, "If we're careful and quick, I think we can escape while the monsters are cleaning up the damage and get home to warn our villages about the invasion." Moving cautiously in single file, you creep down one dark, twisting corridor after another.

Finally you spot an opening in the rock, barely wide enough for an elf to squeeze through.

With your elvensight you can see the opening slopes gently downward. Motioning your party to stay close behind you, you slide into the opening. You travel for a long time before you feel fresh, cool air blowing on your face.

At last, you are outside...free of Shanafria. You will make your way down the mountain to Aralia and warn your people of the coming invasion. With help from Polycanthus and Cambria, you should be able to fend off the invasion and free the Mountain of Mirrors from its evil captors.

You have reached The End of this adventure. Go back to the beginning for another adventure.

You look around at the tons of snow and ice. The way ahead will be difficult. If you turn back, you will probably lose the last chance your village has for survival. Already flakes of the first winter storm are swirling in the cold air.

You make your decision quickly. You will not turn back. You have given your word to do your best and you will succeed or die trying.

Tying the mule to a huge hunk of ice, you set to work. Afterward you can't remember how long it took to clear the trail. Your memory is clouded by the pain of bleeding hands, frozen fingers and snow blind eyes. But at last the job is done...the trail is clear.

You collapse against the shaggy warmth of the mule and fall into an exhausted sleep. At last, you awaken stiff and aching. Rising painfully to your feet, you pull the sleepy, snow-covered mule out onto the narrow trail. It twitches and trembles but follows you nervously along the icy path.

The path is narrow and dangerous. The mountain rises steeply on one side covered in ice and snow. On the other side is the sheer edge of the mountain. At its base, thousands of feet below, are sharp teeth of rock loosely buried in masses of snow and ice brought down by the avalanche.

You edge your way past the snow-covered frost giant's cave. Catching the scent of the dragon, your mule's nostrils flare.

"Easy, boy. I don't like it either. Don't worry, the dragon can't get us now." The mule flattens its ears against its head, but continues to plod through the snow past the cave.

The wind increases. Ice and snow blow against you with tremendous force making it difficult to see and to keep your balance. It is almost impossible to push forward.

Suddenly, the mule rears and begins to scream, jerking hard against the rope. You slip on the icy trail and can no longer control the frightened mule. Screaming wildly, the mule rips the rope from your hands, turns and rushes into the storm. Within seconds, it is lost from sight in the blowing snow. You are alone on the mountain.

You place your hand on the hilt of the Sword of the Magus. As though in answer to your touch, the sword begins to hum. You wonder where the danger could come from in this lonely place.

You draw your sword and peer into the driving storm trying to find your enemy. A figure stumbles toward you out of the whiteness. It's an orc. Its greenish-brown skin is covered with snow. You wonder why it is wandering around outside. Orcs hate the light and usually live underground. You don't have long to wonder... the orc is attacking!

There is a sudden lull in the storm, and a bright ray of sun floods the area. Sensing the strength of the Sword of the Magus and the brilliance of the sun, the orc turns and runs. It rushes down the trail with you following close behind. As you round a bend in the trail, the orc disappears. The snowy trail stretches before you but no footprints mark its surface.

You wonder if possibly orcs have been ambushing the parties who travel through these lonely mountain passes. You know that an orc would be here only for evil purposes.

Great gusts of snow and freezing wind wail past you on the narrow ledge tearing the questions about the orc from your mind. You must soon find shelter or perish.

Closely examining the frozen ground, you see orc footprints leading straight into the side of the mountain. Looking carefully, you discover an opening hidden by over-hanging ledges of snow and icicles. Squeezing between two sheets of ice, you enter an ice cave, sword at the ready for the orc. The Sword of the Magus is silent. Looking down, you see many footprints in the frozen ground. There are footprints of elves, orcs, humans, animals...and some footprints you don't recognize.

You creep slowly into the dark cave. Your elvensight shows you that nothing is in the cave. Slowly you step out of the darkened area. Your feet fly out from under you. You come down hard landing flat on your back. When you land, you begin to slide. This was no small patch of ice. You travel faster and faster, plunging through a tunnel of ice sloping downward.

The walls blur. Slowly, the steep angle of the icy chute begins to even out. Using your feet to brake yourself, you start to slow down. Finally, you skid to a stop, scared and shaken but unhurt.

The Sword of the Magus remains silent. Wherever you are, there are no enemies nearby. Holding the Sword of the Magus before you, you command it, "Great Sword of the Magus, light this place." A clear golden light springs from the sword and fills the area.

You are in a small room made of ice. Behind you, the ice chute rises in shimmering spirals toward the roof far above. You see nothing in the room but the orc footprints leading to a curious door on the far wall. You approach the door slowly, holding the Sword of the Magus before you.

You have never seen a door like this before. It is made from ice and sculpted on it is a great face. Frosty eyebrows jut over deep-set closed eyes. An emormous beak-like nose extends over a bushy ice mustache that bristles with tiny icicles. The mouth is frozen in a frightening snarl.

Stepping up to the door, you push at it with all your strength. It does not move. You back up, rush toward the door, and crash into it with your shoulder. Your arm tingles with pain, but the door hasn't budged.

If you cannot break the door down by force, maybe you can chop your way through it with your axe. You take the axe and bash the door a great blow.

The axe slides in as easily as slicing warm butter but instead of cutting through the door, the door seals around the blade. With difficulty, you pull it free from the ice. This is no ordinary door. It must be enchanted. Still if the orc got though the door, then so can you.

You walk up to the door, raise your hand and knock on its great domed forehead. The sound echoes in the small room.

The door's eyes fly open and glare straight at you. The mouth opens and with a breath like the north wind, it asks, "Who's there?"

A talking door! You stare at it in amazement.

"Well, you went 'knock, knock' and I said 'Who's there?' " says the door. "The least you can do is answer my question. Why are you staring at me? Don't you know it's not polite to stare?" snorts the door. "One meets the worst class of beings down here. Well, I won't waste my time on a dolt who doesn't even know its own name." The eyes blink shut and the door is silent once more.

Your mouth hanging open in amazement, you stare at the door. Your hands hang limply at your sides. You are too astonished to speak. This door is the strangest thing you've ever encountered. If you want answers, you must talk to the door.

Stepping forward boldly, you knock again on the frosty forehead.

The door opens its eyes and asks again, "Who's there?"

This time you have an answer ready. "An elf," you reply.

"An elf, who?" asks the door.

"Elf Landon, from the village of Aralia. Please let me pass, Mr. Door."

The door seems pleased with your answer and says, "That's better. At least you know who you are this time. I'm afraid I can't let you pass. You see it's my job to guard against intruders like you. This is an important place and I have a very important post. I say you can't pass. So go away!"

"Door," you say. "I intend to pass, one way or the other."

"Just try it!" says the door.

1. If you want to attack the door with your axe, turn to page 89.
2. If you want to light your torch and threaten to melt the door, turn to page 69.
3. If you want to use your axe to cut footholds in the ice chute to return to the surface and go home, turn to page 37.

You may find some answers down this corridor. You will have to be very cautious because where there is activity, there is also danger.

You tiptoe along the corridor with your sword drawn, pressing close to the walls alert for danger. You creep through the corridor until you are just at the edge of a brightly-lit opening. Noise is coming from just inside.

Your curiosity overcomes caution. Slipping up to the doorway, you peek in. Bright light streams down from the dome of Shanafria enabling you to see the strange sight below. Hundreds of elves, halflings, and humans are using tools and working in small groups. They are picking and carving their way into the mountain. Enormous piles of dirt, boulders, and rocks litter the landscape.

The prisoners work in a mechanical way not noticing the blows of the monster guards.

Now you know what happened to all the missing travelers. They are being used as slave labor for some kind of mining.

You hear a loud cry. Monsters come running from all over the area. You see furious digging. The prisoners are beaten and threatened until they dig faster. Dirt and rock fly everywhere.

Finally, you see brilliance sparkling in the earth. A large ogre bends down and picks up a handful of something and places it in a large pouch.

It searches the dirt to make sure that everything has been found, then yells at the prisoners to get back to work. Then the ogre calls two goblins over to it and gives them the pouch. The goblins rush away.

These actions puzzle you. Not once did the prisoners fight their captors even though they carry tools which could have been used as weapons. There are far more prisoners than there are guards. All the prisoners are skinny and seem depressed. Why don't they fight?

Suddenly you notice that the goblins sent away by the ogre are climbing the ledge that leads directly to where you are hiding. If they continue on this path, they will find you!

1. If you try to find another hiding place and wait for the goblins to pass, turn to page 136.
2. If you attack the goblins to find out what is in the pouch, turn to page 133.

You shout a warning to the rest of your party. The going is hard but you manage to return to the bank where you began.

You are all exhausted and chilled to the bone from the freezing water. Nigel lounges warm and dry on a mushroom well above the soggy ground. Nervously, he blinks in and out. "I suppose I should have told you before, but I can't stand getting my fur wet. I'm afraid I just couldn't do it."

You lay on the damp ground, limp with exhaustion. After resting a while, you sit up and gather your strength. You must get across the river!

Please turn to page 67 and choose again.

Your curiosity is aroused. You must find out what the monsters are mining. The mining seems to be the reason people have been captured. You hide behind a rock and wait. The goblins appear at the doorway.

"Hold it, Krey. Let me catch my breath. The climb gets tougher every day," says one goblin.

"If you didn't eat so many elves, you wouldn't get so fat and out of shape, Porg," says Krey.

"This bunch should last a while," says Porg as it waddles down the corridor.

They pass the rock where you are hiding. When they disappear into the gloom of the corridor, you spring into action. With two swift blows, you kill both goblins. Bending over their fallen bodies, you pick up the leather pouch.

Returning to the lighted cave opening, you shake out the contents of the leather pouch. Cool and bright, like a handful of stars, you hold a fistful of diamonds. Now you know the secret of Shanafria. Should you return to the cavern and try to stir the prisoners into revolt? The odds are not good. You could go down the staircase and find a way out.

1. If you want to go back to the ledge and down the staircase, turn to page 39.
2. If you want to try to get the prisoners to revolt, turn to page 145.

"We can't help the halfling and we can't finish our mission if we're dead," whispers one of the elves. "Landon, let's get out of here. There has to be another way out."

Sadly, you leave the halfling to his fate and hurriedly push the raft into the river. The raging current seizes it. Unfortunately your earlier bout with the ice floe has damaged the raft. In the middle of the river, it starts to break apart and sink.

Some of the party cling to parts of the raft and are whirled away into the darkness. Others decide to swim for shore. You struggle as the current carries you far away from your friends. The great weight of the Mirror of Souls keeps pulling you under the surface of the frigid waters. You know you won't survive for long. You should have left the Mirror of Souls in the mountain as the Guardians told you.

Nigel watches from the bank. "If they would have waited a little longer, I'm sure they could have made it. Well, at least I'm across. I just know I'm clever enough to find a way out of this terrible place." Looking at the empty river, Nigel heaves a great, sad sigh and settles down to lick the last of the river water from his coat.

You have reached The End of this adventure. Go back to the beginning for another adventure.

You crouch low behind the boulder as the two goblins approach. If you can stay hidden, they won't see you.

"Hold it, Krey!" says one of the goblins. "Let me catch my breath. That climb gets tougher every day."

"If you didn't eat so many elves, you wouldn't get so fat and out of shape, Porg!" says Krey.

"This looks like a good bunch," says Porg, as it waddles down the corridor.

You sigh in relief as the goblin voices fade in the distance. You could follow them at a safe distance and return to the stairs. This could lead to a way out. You wonder if you have a chance to rescue the prisoners from the horde of monsters.

1. If you want to follow the two goblins to the staircase, turn to page 39.
2. If you want to try to rescue the prisoners, turn to page 145.

You persuade your party to have faith in
the Guardians. "They directed me to this
place. They surely knew what would happen.
They didn't say it would be easy. If we succeed with our mission, we will save our
loved ones. They are worth more than our
lives."

"Speak for yourself!" the lynx blurts out.
"I don't think I agree with that. I'm pretty
special. I deserve to live!"

"Be quiet, lynx!" says Desval. "Landon,
you can count on us. Nigel, you're free to go
your own way if you wish."

The lynx walks delicately over to the edge
of the cavern where the water is washing
across the floor. "There doesn't seem to be
much choice. I can either stay here and
drown slowly or leap into that mess and
drown quickly. I might as well stay here.
This might just work out. Then I'd be a hero.
If anyone deserves to be a hero, it's me!"

Ignoring the water lapping at your feet,
everyone crowds around the Mirror of Souls.
Even Nigel stops complaining. Dramatic
changes are taking place. Before you, the
clouds still roll in the sky. The thunder and
lightning have gotten even worse.

Great flashes of blinding light and booming blasts of thunder continue to echo from one side of the mountain to the other. Rain falls in thick sheets. You see great chunks of the collapsed pillar in the river.

The freezing water slowly rises to knee level. Nigel has found a large boulder and perches hunched on top of it. His fur is ruffled angrily and his gold eyes shoot darts of displeasure at everyone.

Staring intently into the pelting rain, you see a blurry form. The form moves closer... it's the frost giant! Drenched by the rain, it stands like a giant statue. It is gathering the monsters together and urging them forward. Soon, a solid wall of monsters is moving shoulder-to-shoulder through the downpour toward you.

You cannot fight such an attack. The only escape is the river... and that looks like certain death. Fear is on everyone's face. You look at each other in despair.

The monsters draw ever closer. Soon, they will reach you. The icy water now reaches your waist. The violent current tugs at you and draws you ever closer to the whirlpool.

Suddenly, you hear a crash louder than any you've ever heard. It sounds like the world is ending.

The noise thunders on and on without end. The air is choked with ice particles and dust. You can see nothing.

You look down. Incredibly the water is subsiding. It drains down to your knees... your ankles... the floor. It drains off rapidly, leaving the floor glistening with moisture. The Mirror of Souls lies on the floor, knocked ff its base.

Cautiously, not understanding what has happened, everyone, even Nigel, creeps to the edge of the cavern and looks out.

Below you is a deep, black hole swirling away beneath the mountain. It is the bed of the whirlpool, now empty of water. Stretching before you as far as the eye can see is a field of ice. Great, jagged chunks of ice cover what once was the interior of Shanafria.

Everything...the pillar...the frost giant...
the monsters...the river...probably even the
Guardians...is covered by the fallen dome.
The stone walls of the mountain base hold
the shattered dome like a great bowl holding ice chips. The brilliant sun shines down
on the glittering ice.

You've done it! The mission is a success!
Your loved ones and your homes are saved!
"See, I told you everything would be all
right!" says Nigel. Fresh air sweeps into the
cavern.

Desval grasps the Mirror of Souls to his
chest. "Let's leave. We've done what the
Guardians wanted. We didn't get any diamonds for ourselves but the Mirror of Souls
is big enough for all of us. We should get
some reward from all this struggle."

"We cannot do that," you say firmly. "I
promised the Guardians that we would
leave the Mirror of Souls in the mountain."

"They couldn't have survived the fall of
the dome. Why should you keep that promise now?" asks Desval. "I say we keep it and
get out of here. We can walk across the ice
field, climb the mountain, and be home before dark."

"A promise is a promise," says one of the humans. "Thanks to Guardians, we fulfilled the mission and survived. I say we do what Landon says. Leave the Mirror of Souls here and leave by way of the whirlpool tunnel."

Your party is undecided. Should you believe that the Guardians are dead, take the Mirror of Souls, and break your promise? Or should you honor your promise, regardless of the fate of the Guardians?

1. If you want to take the Mirror of Souls, turn to page 68.
2. If you want to leave the Mirror of Souls, turn to page 147.

Your party votes to try to rescue the help-less halfling. The lynx refuses to help say-ing, "I see quite enough of those monsters without going into the middle of them. No, thank you very much but I'll stay right here. Do let me know how everything turns out." With that, he begins to groom his fur and pointedly ignores all of you as you creep over the bank and edge your way to the monster's camp. You move very quietly, dodging like shadows from rock to rock. Suddenly, you are discovered and sur-rounded by monsters.

"Hey, look! We got visitors!" shouts an orc. Rough hands grab at you and wrench you from your hiding place. You are thrown from orc to orc. The world spins crazily. Hideous visions whirl by...camp fires...leer-ing monsters...icy ground...the ice pillar ringed by piles of flashing diamonds...Fang, the white dragon.

In the midst of a shout of laughter, you are dumped beside the sad halfling. Two of your companions are tossed in next to you. Fang is almost upon you...pulling out your weapons, you stagger to your feet, deter-mined to fight.

Fang's huge head snakes out. You swing the Sword of the Magus at its neck. Your blade bounces off the armor-like scales. Fang snatches you in its claws. Slowly, beating the air with its wings to gain altitude, the dragon rises.

As you rise steadily higher, you see below the fabulous diamonds heaped at the base of the ice pillar. You see your friends being bound and led away by the monsters. You kick and flail at Fang helplessly. It's no use... Fang doesn't even feel your blows. Unless you can think of some way to escape, you will soon be a dragon's dinner.

You have reached The End of this adventure. Go back to the beginning for another adventure.

Feeling as though you will be spotted at any moment, you creep out on the ledge. Moving as quickly as possible, you slither down to the floor of the cavern. You have not been seen.

Every eye in the place is directed at only one thing... the mining.

You are able to sneak up on a goblin guard and slay it. Running up to the group of prisoners, you yell, "I've come to rescue you. Pick up your tools and follow me!" Without checking to see if they are following you, you rush off.

You choose an ogre as your next target. Your blows only make it insanely angry for it wears armor underneath its leather shirt. It turns to face you.

"Attack! Attack!" you yell. No one comes to your aid. Attracted by the noise, other monsters join the ogre. They advance toward you.

You look around frantically for help. The prisoners you rescued still stand where you left them. They have not moved.

You are now ringed by monsters. They disarm you easily. The ogre you attacked chains you to the prisoners. It kicks you in the ribs.

"Attack me, will you? You'll be sorry. Start digging. No tools for you. Use your hands since you're so tough!" the ogre taunts.

You look around but all you see are the vacant, staring eyes of the prisoners. No one will aid or comfort you. You will learn the secret of Shanafria but it doesn't seem likely that information will do you or your village any good.

You have reached The End of this adventure. Go back to the beginning for another adventure.

"No, I promised the Guardians that we would leave the Mirror of Souls in the mountain. Whether they still live is not the question. I promised I would leave the diamond here. If I break my word, it doesn't matter if anyone knows it. I'll know it."

Your party grumbles a little, but no one disagrees with you. With great respect, you place the Mirror of Souls gently on the floor of the cave before you. After one last, longing glance at its beautiful face, everyone files from the cavern.

It is not as difficult to leave as it was to enter. Many large chunks of ice rest against the sides of the mountain wall. Nigel leaps down to the riverbed in graceful bounds, forgetting this once his dislike of getting wet. The rest of you carefully pick your way down to the edge of the empty whirlpool.

Centuries of raging water and grinding ice have carved this huge funnel out of solid rock. It is hard to believe all the water is gone. Gingerly, you lower yourself into the pit.

It is very dark. You open your backpack and pull out your torches and tinder box and hand them to your friends. Very soon, you are on your way, your path lit by smoking, flickering torches. You command the Sword of the Magus to light and its golden light adds to the torchlight.

The dry bed of the whirlpool stretches before you. You are under Shanafria. Pools of water remind you that not long ago this dark tunnel was filled with raging waters.

An unexpected trickle of water starts to flow down the tunnel. Slowly the flow increases. The river could break through the tunnel and flood it once more. Everyone in your party is thinking the same thing. You rush through the tunnel as the flow of freezing water rapidly increases.

A bend lies just ahead of you. As you turn the corner, a blast of cold air stuns you and a clear light glares in your eyes. You must be close to the end of the tunnel.

Below you lies a rock staircase strewn with ice left by the swirling waters. Large lumps of ice and snow choke the opening. You stand at the opening drinking in the sun and the fresh air. You feel safe and happy. Your mission has been a success!

You are about to begin the long climb
when you hear the tiny voice of one of the
Guardians say, "Well done, Landon. We
share thy joy. To reward thee and thy brave
friends, please accept these tokens of our
gratitude."

One of the ice knobs ringing the mouth of
the river bed moves. There shining in the
snow, you see a mound of glittering diamonds, each the size of a hen's egg.

"These are not ordinary diamonds. They
possess special powers. When their owners
hold them, they can look deep into the
hearts of others. They will tell thee if the
person is honorable and truthful. These are
precious gifts. Use them well. Farewell,
Landon. You have done us and your people
a great service."

Each of your party chooses a diamond. As you start down the icy staircase, you hear a tremendous roar. Large chunks of ice and torrents of water have burst through the tunnel and start to pour down the staircase.

You leap for the safety of the snowy slopes... you make it!! You and your party stand and watch the roaring waters as they rage past. The last entrance to Shanafria is now sealed.

You make your way to the foot of Shanafria. Elves, halflings, and humans separate to make their way home. The parting makes you sad, but you know you will always keep the memories of your quest in your heart even though you may never see most of your friends again.

"I better tag along with you, Landon," says Nigel. "Wouldn't want to see you get lost. After all, you never would have made it without me."

"You know, we could get one of Aralia's goldsmiths to put this diamond on a chain for me to wear around my neck. This diamond is one of the few things I've seen that's good enough to be worn next to my handsome fur. Don't you agree?"

Still chattering happily to himself, Nigel trots briskly at your side as you and your fellow elves start the journey home.

The End. Go back to the beginning and start the book again.